Pacific Coast
Bird Finder

a pocket guide to some frequently seen birds

by Roger J. Lederer, Ph.D.

Professor of Biological Sciences
California State University, Chico

illustrated by Jacquelyn S. Giuffré

How much can a pocket-sized book do?

This book will help you to know and identify 61 frequently seen birds in this area.

To identify *all* of the 500 or so bird species found on the Pacific coast, you'll need a larger, complete field guide such as:

Birds of North America (A Guide to Field Identification),
    by Robbins, Bruun, Zim, and Singer. Golden Press.

A *Field Guide to Western Birds,* by R. T. Peterson. 2nd ed.
    Peterson Field Guide Series. Houghton Mifflin Co.

For general information about Pacific coast birds we suggest:

The Birds of California, by A. Small. Winchester Press.
Birds of the Pacific Northwest, by Gabrielson and Jewett. Dover Press.
The Audubon Illustrated Handbook of American Birds, by E. M. Reilly.
    McGraw-Hill.

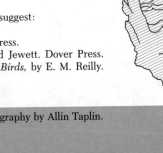

To find the birds you're most likely to see, pick a symbol below for the habitat you are in. Then flip through the book to the pages with green on the outer margin at the level of that symbol here.

How to use this book

If, for example, you're in a forest, look at pages with green near the bottom of the right- or left-hand margin.

Dark green margin marks and symbols indicate the usual habitat of each bird. Additional but less typical habitats a bird may also live in are shown in light green.

Heavy green lines represent six inches (length of this page) to scale of illustration.

— six inches —————▶

Standardized names are given first with alternate names in parentheses.

Ocean	shores of the Pacific — beaches and bluffs	
Lakes and Streams	open freshwater — deep or shallow	
Marshes	shallow freshwater with tules, cattails, etc. (including ricefields)	
Prairies	grasslands, fields of grain, other crops	
Farms, Parks and Cities	areas most affected by civilization	
Woods	open woods, mostly oak or pine	
Forests	dense, evergreen, conifer forests	

Pelicans

Catch fish in flexible, scoop-like throat pouch and hooked beak, turn fish in pouch to swallow head first. Feet are webbed. Fish in flocks and nest in colonies along shore. Lay two or three eggs in simple ground nest made of vegetation. May flutter throat pouches to cool themselves in hot weather. Sometimes grunt or croak.

Brown Pelican has whitish head, lives only on seacoast, and fishes by diving from air. Before DDT ban, reproduction was dangerously hampered by eggshell thinning and premature breakage due to cumulative effect of insecticide in diet.

White Pelican has black wingtips, lives mainly on inland lakes, and fishes by diving from water surface.

Double-crested Cormorant

Black except for orange face and throat. The most common and widespread fish-eating cormorant. Also found far inland.

Like closely related pelicans, cormorants make ground nest on rocky shores and islands. Fish in groups and fly close to water in straight-line flock. Often stand on shore with wings spread to dry water-logged feathers.

Excellent swimmers. Japanese fishermen send five or six into water leashed together with neck rings to prevent swallowing, then haul them in and empty their throats of fish.

Similar **Brant's Cormorant** has blue throat. Smaller **Pelagic Cormorant** has red face and white patch on side.

Herring Gull

Bill is rounded above, back is light-colored, legs pink. Sits higher in water than other floating birds. "Seagulls" range far inland, are memorialized for eating a cricket plague in Utah. Eat almost anything live or dead. Unlike diving birds they keep inner feathers dry and thus don't soak up spilled oil. Build ground nests on rocky lake shores, islands or cliff ledges. Two or three young hatch and peck at red spot on lower part of parent's bill. Parent responds by regurgitating food.

Other Pacific coast gulls:

Western—dark back, pink legs

California—light back, yellow-green legs

Ring-billed—black ring around yellow bill

Bonaparte's—black head, fast, tern-like flight

Immature gulls are mottled brown and gray, difficult to tell apart.

Black Tern ⑤

Black and gray. Related to gulls, but smaller, with longer, thinner wings and a straight, pointed bill. Graceful flight over water becomes erratic due to frequent turning to see into water for fish. May hover before diving. Do not sit on water. Aggressive in defending floating nest of reeds. May dive at and pull hair of human intruders.

Other commonly seen terns are **Forster's** and **Caspian.** Both are white with black cap. Caspian is twice as large, with red bill.

Grebes

Grebes are excellent divers and underwater swimmers. Feed on fish and other water animals in lakes, marshes and ponds. Lobed feet are set far back on body for swimming. Adjust buoyancy to float low or high in water by trapping air between body feathers or compressing feathers to expel it.

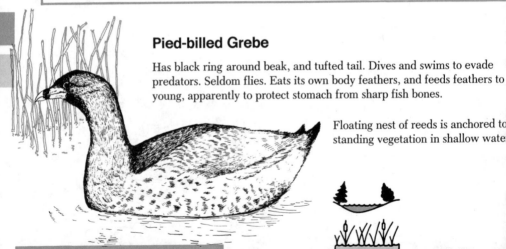

Pied-billed Grebe

Has black ring around beak, and tufted tail. Dives and swims to evade predators. Seldom flies. Eats its own body feathers, and feeds feathers to young, apparently to protect stomach from sharp fish bones.

Floating nest of reeds is anchored to standing vegetation in shallow water

Western Grebe

Winters along entire U.S. Pacific coast, but breeds from there eastward to Minnesota on inland lakes, in colonies up to several thousand pairs. Lays three or four eggs in floating nest of tules.

In courtship, breeding pairs, or two males, swim side-by-side making head-turning movements and occasional dives. Suddenly both will rise straight up and literally run across water. Dance often ends with simultaneous dive.

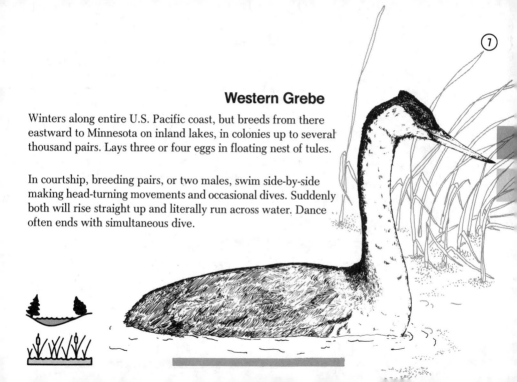

Belted Kingfisher

Shaggy, big-headed, blue and white. Gives a long, chattering call in flight. Selects a streamside perch with good view and waits for fish to dive on. May swim briefly to catch prey. Beats fish on branch to kill it, then swallows it head first so fins won't get stuck.

Usually alone except in breeding season. Defends narrow territory along stream. Lays about seven eggs in streamside burrow dug with feet and beak. Eggs are white. Hidden in burrow, they need no camouflage.

Has dark brown spots on white breast, and high-pitched peep. Feeds along water's edge on small animals. Runs in short spurts, bobs up and down like a see-saw, but rarely walks. Flies in alternate bursts of quick flapping and long glides. Lays four spotted, well camouflaged eggs in crude nest or depression in ground, often on gravel or under a rock ledge.

Frequent bobbing (apart from courtship bobbing done with outstretched wings) may provide per-spective to judge distance (like rattlesnake weaving before strike).

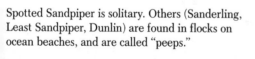

Spotted Sandpiper is solitary. Others (Sanderling, Least Sandpiper, Dunlin) are found in flocks on ocean beaches, and are called "peeps."

Egrets

The only all white marsh birds on Pacific coast. Almost exterminated around 1900 when feathers were prized for decorating women's hats. May eat mice, fish, frogs, crayfish, and the like.

Great Egrets have yellow bills and raise two or three young in tree rookeries. Smaller Snowy Egrets have black bills and nest in marshes on platforms of vegetation, or shrubs.

Great Blue Heron

Blue-gray, up to four feet tall. Common throughout U.S. Raises young in tree rookeries, on ground, or alone. Flexible neck has about 20 vertebrae. Oil gland is poorly developed, but uses talcum-like, disintegrated tips of "powder-down" breast feathers for waterproofing. Squawks angrily when disturbed.

Long-Legged Marsh Birds

Herons, egrets and bitterns wade slowly or stand waiting to stab with long neck and beak at passing fish, frogs, crayfish, etc. They launch into flight from "springboard" legs, and flap slowly off with neck pulled in and feet trailing. Raccoons may raid nests, but natural enemies are few. Herons and Great Egrets often nest together in tree colonies called rookeries, using large, twiggy nests.

American Bittern

Tan and white-streaked to blend with usual background of marsh plants. Hard for predators to find and approach when standing still, beak straight up—a position which allows 360 degree vision from eyes on sides of head. May take crouching, spread-winged defensive posture when approached, but more often leaps off with the bellow of a bullfrog. Similarly voiced European relative is called "marsh cow."

⑫ Killdeer

Has dark brown cap; wide brown face band; white underparts except for two dark breast bands; brown back; pointed wings; rusty tail and rump. Call is high, shrill "kill-deer, kill-deer," A common freshwater shore bird. Also found in almost all open habitats. Finds invertebrates to eat along shore and on ground.

Nest on ground is often only a depression in gravel. Arranges four eggs with small ends inward to prevent rolling. May replace missing egg with rock to keep others in place.

Young are speckled like eggs for camouflage. On approac of predator they sit still and inconspicious while parents scream and run with drooping wing to feign injury and divert intruder's attention from nest.

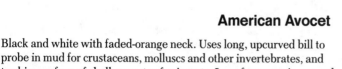

American Avocet

Black and white with faded-orange neck. Uses long, upcurved bill to probe in mud for crustaceans, molluscs and other invertebrates, and to skim surface of shallow water for insects. Lays four eggs in ground depression lined with vegetation. Pairs bow and preen during courtship ritual.

Closely related **Black-necked Stilt** has similar but straighter bill with neck white in front, black in back.

⑭ Red-winged Blackbird

Black with bright-red shoulder patch on male. Found in marshes throughout North America. Eats insects. Winters in warmer regions in separate all-male and all-female colonies. Males reach spring breeding grounds first and establish territories from which they drive out other males. Females arrive and select mate with territory—one to three females to each male. Each female builds a nest made of tules in standing tules or cattails. Four eggs per nest.

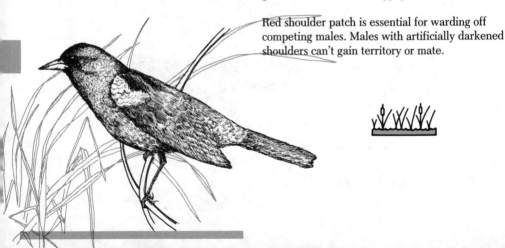

Red shoulder patch is essential for warding off competing males. Males with artificially darkened shoulders can't gain territory or mate.

Black except for white on wing edges and bill. Lobed feet for paddling. Very common in all open water. Walks with waddle. Must run on top of water or over land to take off with stubby wings. Running often makes flight unnecessary. Lays six or seven eggs on mat of floating vegetation. Young swim soon after hatching, are fed on parents' usual diet of aquatic organisms and vegetation.

Name derives from "soot" color.

A disappointment to hunters.
Too easy to shoot,
too hard to eat.

(15)
American Coot
(Mudhen, Whitebill)

Swans, geese, and the ducks shown here have:

- a flat "duck" bill to grasp and strain submerged vegetation, with a specially sensitive "lip" to identify food textures.

- a layer of fat and down feathers for warmth in icy water. Fat and down thicken in winter.

- precocial young that walk soon after hatching. Ground nesters must flee predators.

- migration. As frozen marshes open in spring thaw, they leave crowded winter waters and risk long journeys to seek abundant food needed for breeding.

- v-formation flight. To avoid turbulent wake of other fowl and to keep flock within horizontally oriented field of vision, they fly to one side and at the same level. Flock leadership rotates.

- necks extended in flight. Swans have longest necks and slowest wingbeat. Duck necks are shortest, and their wingbeat is too fast to count.

Male has striking, multicolored head, red eyes, flowing nape feathers. More common in eastern U.S. Unlike most other ducks, it nests in tree cavities (or artificial nest boxes) but has, nevertheless, some waterfowl habits which seem more appropriate to ground nesting. Adults fly into nest head first without perching. Fluffy young ones are precocial. They climb from the nest before learning to fly, and tumble softly to the ground. (Female is reported to carry young to ground on back.)

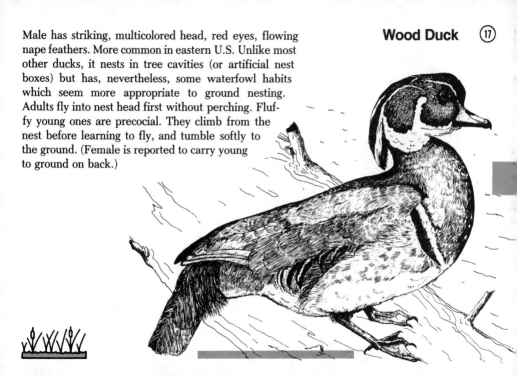

(18) Mallard

Males have green head, white neck ring, and cinnamon chest. Female is brown-streaked. Both sexes have purple-iridescent wing patch bordered by white. The best known duck. Has a resounding, classical "quack." Many barnyard ducks are domesticated versions of Mallard. Can take off almost vertically from water.

Lays 10 to 15 eggs in down-lined nest on ground, usually well concealed by vegetation.

The ducks shown here feed on submerged vegetation by paddling with their webbed feet to keep head down and tail up. This is called dabbling.

Male has white chest, strip of white running up neck, and long, pointed tail. Female is drab, mottled brown. Lays 7 to 12 eggs in simple grass nest on ground. Winter flocks of thousands gather in wildlife refuges of California Central Valley. Prized by hunters who call it "sprig." Whistles.

Whistling Swan

Large and white. Deep, resonant honk results from coils in long windpipe at base of neck which has 25 vertebrae. Does not really whistle. Dabbles, but also eats grass in fields. Winters in California Central Valley and breeds in arctic tundra.

Largest number of feathers counted on any bird was about 25,000 on a Whistling Swan. Swan groups are called herds.

Dark except for white patches on chin, face and tail. Found throughout U.S., but especially in California Central Valley during winter.

Breeds in Canada, northern U.S. (northern California). Feeds on grasses, grains and aquatic insects. Lays five or six eggs in ground nest. Also known to nest in trees. Young goslings follow parents and learn what to eat. Honking is more raspy than Swan call.

Several races exist, including small "cacklers" and large "honkers."

㉒ Ring-necked Pheasant

Male (most often seen) has red face, purple head and iridescent color over body. Female is brown, drab, avoids detection. Often polygamous. Lays 10-15 eggs in simple ground nest. Several females may lay and abandon 50 or more eggs in "dump" nest (reason unknown). Short wings and stocky body make it a poor flier, but it can crouch, run and fly short distances to avoid enemies and entertain hunters. Diet includes insects and seeds.

Introduced from Asia and naturalized here, especially in grasslands.

Male has black chin, gray breast; female is brownish. Both have black plume on forehead. Inhabits brushy ground. Call is low, whistled "chi-ca-go." In flocks except when paired for breeding. Lays about 15 eggs in simple ground nest. Water in diet (seeds, grain, berries, greenery) is sufficient. Doesn't need to drink. Legally hunted. California state bird.

California Quail
(Valley Quail)

You'll find **Gambel's Quail** in deserts (white belly with black spot) and the **Mountain Quail** in mountains (brown throat and belly, very long-thin plume).

Grain Eaters

Quail, pheasants, turkeys and chickens are related, and have equipment for digesting hard seeds and grain. Lower neck has expansible crop to store quickly gobbled food for slow grinding in muscular part of stomach (gizzard) which contains swallowed gravel (grit). They run fast, fly laboriously with short wings.

Marsh Hawk   (Harrier)

Males are gray, females tan. Both display obvious white rump
in typical low flight over marshes, meadows, croplands seeking
small rodents. Males can pass food to females in flight. Lays
four to six eggs in nest of grass and reeds built on platform of
twigs and tules in marsh or meadow.

Adapted to hunting over tall, dense marsh vegetation. Other
hawks searching over dry-land vegetation can profit by soaring
high to view wide area from many angles, but Marsh Hawk's
effective field of vision is narrowed to single, vertical channel
by tules, high grass, cattails, etc. Since prey is visible only
when directly underneath, nothing would be gained by high
soaring. Also, cooler marshes have fewer updrafts.

(Sparrow Hawk)

The smallest American hawk. Tail is rust-colored, head has patterned face. Very common. Often seen in open, sitting on poles or wires waiting to spot its prey: small rodents, large insects, lizards, sitting birds.

Resembles much larger Red-tailed Hawk except that it doesn't soar. Instead it flies actively and often hovers over prey before diving.

Nests in tree cavities, barns, buildings. Lays three eggs.

Turkey Vulture

(Buzzard, Turkey Buzzard)

Naked head is red, turkey-like; body dark brown, funereal. Resembles hawks and eagles in circular soaring, but has smaller-looking head, more v-shaped silhouette, and somewhat narrower tail. Eats dead animals. Frequents highways, looking for road kills—one of few birds that may have sense of smell. Wards off attackers by vomiting. Flocks gather for fall migration. Departure is triggered by change in length of day, predictable. (See Barn Swallow.) Hinkley, Ohio, celebrates annual February return on Buzzard Day. Lays two eggs on ground or in tree cavity. No nest. Related to California Condor and Black Vulture of southwestern U.S.

Red-tailed Hawk ㉗

The most commonly seen hawk. Only adults have rust-colored tail, but all ages have dark, contrasting band across belly. Body darkness varies. Often seen soaring over meadows and woods when sun makes thermal updrafts, or waiting on posts and poles in cloudy weather. Uses excellent vision to spot rodents to grasp in powerful talons and tear apart with hooked beak. Young may cover captured prey with outspread wings to avoid sharing with nestmates, etc. Build large, open tree nests.

Ecological value in rodent control vastly outweighs rare chicken taken by hawks, but ignorant gunning kills many "chicken hawks" despite Federal and State protection.

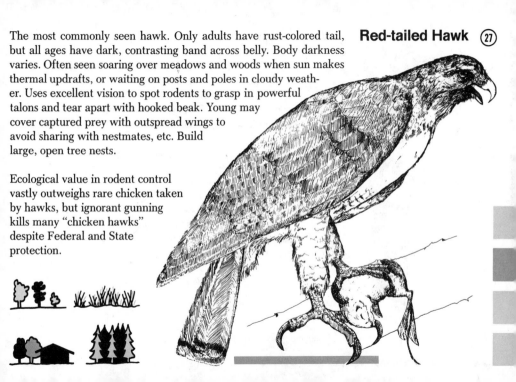

(28)

Western Kingbird

Yellow belly, black tail. Common along rural roadsides perched on wires and fences. Diet is largely flying insects caught by darting out from ambush. Beats large or hard-bodied insects against branch to soften them before swallowing. May also beat prey to avoid being stung. Also eats berries.

Lays three to five eggs in simple grassy nest placed on horizontal tree limb.

Very aggressive. Often seen chasing larger, but less agile hawks and crows. Such harassment forces predatory birds to hunt elsewhere. Kingbirds (also flocks of other small birds) can do this safely because they are vulnerable to predatory birds (except falcons) only when sitting.

Barn Swallow

The only swallow with long, forked tail. Metallic-blue above with rusty forehead, throat and belly. Song is pleasant, sustained twittering. Excellent, graceful flier, but barely able to walk. Eats only insects caught in flight, often by dipping into surface of water. Large groups feed over water or perch on wires in spring and fall. Nest in colonies of up to several hundred, placing grass- or feather-lined nests made of mud and straw in, on, or under eaves of farm buildings and bridges.

Cliff Swallows make similar nests, but use only mud and add entrance tunnel. **Bank** and **Rough-winged Swallows** use river-bank burrows. **Tree** and **Violet-green Swallows** use tree cavities.

Migration is triggered by change in length of day and begins within week or so of same date. Arrival may spread over longer period as weather affects rate of travel.

Brown-headed Cowbird

Male has black body, brown head; female is gray-ish-brown all over. Coloring is dull. Call is weak, high-pitched whistle. Found especially in pastures where cattle stir up insects that birds feed on.

The only North American nest parasite. Lays 10 to 15 eggs, each in a separate nest of another bird—most often warblers, finches, vireos, and flycatchers. (Over a hundred species parasitized.) May remove other birds' eggs. Other birds then hatch egg and raise alien chick as one of their own. Nestmates may starve when young cowbird is larger and hogs food. Apparently adopted parents are not always fooled. Nests have been found with unhatched cowbird egg layered over with a new bottom. Birdnests must be poor schools, since cowbirds never learn to act like warblers, finches, etc.

Yellow-billed Magpie

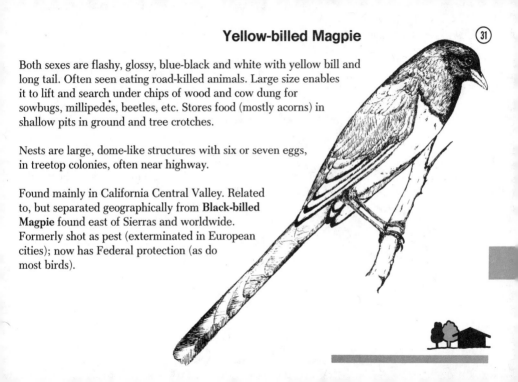

Both sexes are flashy, glossy, blue-black and white with yellow bill and long tail. Often seen eating road-killed animals. Large size enables it to lift and search under chips of wood and cow dung for sowbugs, millipedes, beetles, etc. Stores food (mostly acorns) in shallow pits in ground and tree crotches.

Nests are large, dome-like structures with six or seven eggs, in treetop colonies, often near highway.

Found mainly in California Central Valley. Related to, but separated geographically from **Black-billed Magpie** found east of Sierras and worldwide. Formerly shot as pest (exterminated in European cities); now has Federal protection (as do most birds).

③② Brewer's Blackbird

Male is glossy black with yellow eye; female is brownish with brown eye. Resembles cowbird except for darker head and narrower bill. Nests in tops of small trees or in urban hedges.

Pairs tend to stay together even in flocks. Polygamous in years when food supply is abundant.

Important in control of plant-eating insects. Often feeds in large flocks with all birds moving in same direction. Flocks seem to roll as birds in rear fly to front. By foraging systematically they benefit from each other's food discoveries and can warn each other of predators.

Black with rounded tail. Call is loud "caw-caw." Migrates, Winter flocks may number in millions. Abused for ages, crows avoid people. Now protected by Federal law because benefit from insects and mice eaten far outweighs any crop damage by crows. Also useful scavengers. Often prey on small birds and their eggs.

Crows don't sing to defend territory. They hold none permanently. Flock living makes song to attract mate unnecessary. Yet crows are songbirds, have necessary vocal equipment and can be taught to "talk" in captivity.

Flocks can be driven off by broadcasting recorded crow distress signals.

Ravens are larger and have wedge-shaped tails.

㉞ Rock Dove

Color varies. City pigeons are sooty, have nest sites which resemble rocky cliffs of original European habitat. Prefer grain, but may accept almost any food. Nest up to six times a year. Droppings "whitewash" statues, etc. May transmit disease, ornithosis (psittacosis) to humans. Handlers of recent dead city pigeons may "adopt" lice. Since ancient Egypt, domestic pigeons have been bred into wide variety, including homers, carriers, racers, and laboratory pigeons.

Birds of Civilization

Pigeon, Starling and House Sparrow are highly adapted to human-dominated environment of cities and farms. They stuff simple nests in eaves, ledges, rafters; thrive on varied diet of whatever food is available; proliferate for lack of natural predators; are hard to eradicate; and occupy a niche in urban ecology as do crabgrass, Ailanthus trees, rats and roaches.

Starlings have blue-black body with metallic sheen and a shorter tail than other black birds. In spring, black bill turns yellow and old feathers wear off to expose white spots. Gives series of high whistles, also mimics (akin to Mynahs). Introduced to New York because mentioned by Shakespeare; on Pacific coast since 1940's. Large pesty winter flocks are sometimes dispersed by broadcasting Starling distress calls. Eats insects, but also corn and cattle feed.

House Sparrows chirp noisily—no song. Male has black face mask, eyestripe and nape. Female is plain brown. Introduced in U.S. in late 1800's by governments, co-ops, and immigrants seeking reminder of Europe. Competing birds shot in New York's Central Park. Philadelphia paid first to establish and later to eradicate them. Major predator is domestic cat. May nest in street lights. More akin to brightly colored weaverbirds of Africa and Asia than to other sparrows. Does not migrate.

Starling

House Sparrow

(English Sparrow)

Finches

These sparrow-like seed eaters often visit bird feeders. They often sing in their undulating flight.

American Goldfinch shown here is bright yellow with black cap and wings (often called wild canary). It often flocks together, especially in winter, with **Lesser Goldfinch** which has a greenish back.

The brownish, streaked **House Finch** (mistakenly called linnet) has an overlaid color of dull red and a very melodious, warbling song which ends with a buzz.

(summer)

Male has black-and-white-striped head.
Very common in low-elevation wooded
areas, parklands and backyards during winter. Forages on ground and in low shrubs
for seeds, grain and insects. Winter flocks
often include **Golden-crowned Sparrows**
with bright yellow crown bordered by black.

Migrates in summer to far north and high elevations where it nests on ground in tundra. One
population nests in coastal scrub lands of the west.

Plaintive, fluctuating whistle has been well stud-
ied. Artificially isolated young develop private
song, but must hear adult models to learn typical
White-Crown song. There are local dialects in
Berkeley, Santa Monica, elsewhere.

(winter)

Evening Grosbeak

Heavy-bodied, yellow, white and black. Breeds mainly in northern coniferous forests of U.S. and Canada. Winters in large flocks on Pacific coast where it relishes sunflower seeds placed in bird feeders.

Heavy bill can crack open pine nuts and tough seed other birds can't manage. The similar European Hawfinch can crack olive pits with a force which has been measured at 159 pounds.

(summer)

(winter)

Generally grayish brown with pink bill and white belly. Head and neck are darker (often black, like an executioner's hood). Breeds in northern coniferous forests. Winters on Pacific coast. Hops around brush piles searching for seeds and occasional insects. Related to like-sized sparrows and finches.

Display of flashy white outer tail feathers may help flying juncos to stay in sight of each other. In landing, white feathers are folded under. Perhaps this prevents detection by predators such as falcons, hawks, foxes.

(winter)

Rufous-sided Towhee (Spotted Towhee)

Has black head, white chest and belly, rusty (rufous) sides and spotted wings. Eats insects, seeds.

Abundant in brushy areas where it is more often heard than seen. Call is often a buzz.

Towhees speak with geographic accents. Variants of Rufous-sided Towhee are known as Arctic, Spurred, Texas, Nevada, Oregon, Sacramento, San Francisco, San Diego, San Clemente, Cape Colnett, Guadalupe and Large-billed Towhee.

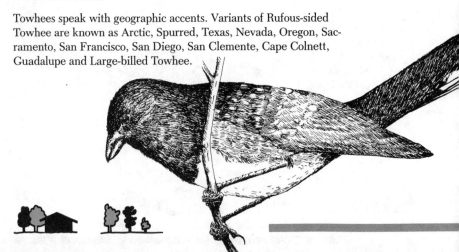

Cedar Waxwing

Has permanent topknot, smooth, silky-looking feathers, and several feather tips on each wing that appear to have been dipped in red sealing wax (function unknown). Most often seen in winter coastal-urban habitat where flocks (often with Robins) systematically strip red berries from pyracantha bushes (pictured). Fermented berries are said to make them drunk, but story lacks evidence. Diet includes insects. Flocking waxwings emit soft whistling sounds. Breed in coniferous forests of Canada and Pacific northwest.

 (summer)

 (winter)

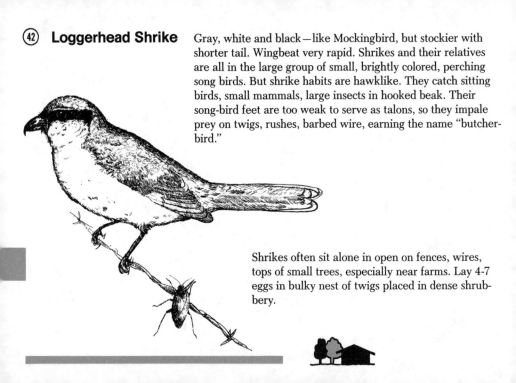

(42) **Loggerhead Shrike**

Gray, white and black—like Mockingbird, but stockier with shorter tail. Wingbeat very rapid. Shrikes and their relatives are all in the large group of small, brightly colored, perching song birds. But shrike habits are hawklike. They catch sitting birds, small mammals, large insects in hooked beak. Their song-bird feet are too weak to serve as talons, so they impale prey on twigs, rushes, barbed wire, earning the name "butcher-bird."

Shrikes often sit alone in open on fences, wires, tops of small trees, especially near farms. Lay 4-7 eggs in bulky nest of twigs placed in dense shrubbery.

Gray, Robin-sized, with white wing patches. Sings at night. Mimics and "mocks" other birds with a wide repertoire. Lays four pale blue eggs with brown splotches in bulky, twiggy nest in dense shrubbery. Eats berries, seed, insects. Rare north of California.

Many birds sing to clear their territories of competing members of their own species. Mockingbird imitations may be accurate enough to fool and drive away other species as well. Experiments show imitations are learned, not instinctive. Flashing displays of white wing patches may also drive off intruders.

(44) The most commonly seen owl. Light brown and white with heart-shaped face. Li[ke] distantly related hawks, preys mostly on rodents. Searches at night over prairi[es] and farms using night vision which far exceeds that of humans. Feather-covere[d] asymmetrical ears, which look human under feathers, can sense direction a[nd] pinpoint source of sound. Head can turn almost full circle. Fringed wi[ng] feathers produce silent flight. Unlike most birds which hatch young [in] even-aged groups, owl nests contain young of varying ages. Young m[ay] leave nest early and require care until they can fly. Young found [on] ground have seldom been abandoned, and are extremely hard [to] raise in captivity. Look under roosting trees for compacte[d] regurgitated "owl pellets" which contain complete skeleto[ns] and fur of one or more small animals—a record of owl di[et.]

Barn Owl

(White-faced Owl, Monkey-faced Owl)

Common Nighthawk (45)

(Bullbat)

Variously brown and white to blend with ground or tree limb. A hawk in name only. Feet are too weak for walking. Lies along horizontal branch instead of perching. Most active at dawn and dusk, expertly swooping to catch flying insects in huge, gaping mouth. No nest. Lays two camouflaged eggs on rocky surface (sometimes gravel roof). Call is long, raspy "beep." In spring courtship display it circles high, dives, pulls out with feathers spread to produce fog-horn sound. Akin to southwestern Poorwill—one of the very few hibernating birds.

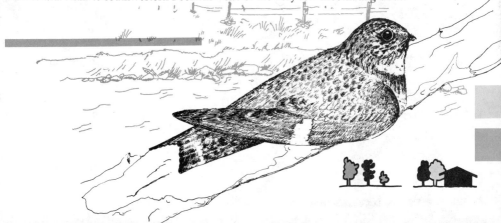

Common Flicker

A large woodpecker. Male has black or red "moustache" behind bill. Color under wing is usually red, but may be yellow, as in eastern U.S. flickers, or orange. Displays white rump in flight. Often probes ground for food. The most likely woodpecker to become a pest by pounding holes in roofs.

Hairy Woodpecker

Black and white except for red pa on back of male's head. Distinctiv white back shows between black wings. Lays three to six eggs on chipped wood at bottom of nest ca ity carved by both parents. Simila but smaller **Downy Woodpecker** i habits lower-elevation woods and parks.

Acorn Woodpecker

Back of head is red. Displays white wing patches and rump in flight. Lives in large groups which raise young cooperatively and share "granaries"—old trees, poles, buildings they riddle with holes to hold acorns and nuts tightly, safe from squirrels, crows, etc. They transfer drying, shrinking nuts to tighter holes, and eventually crack shells to extract nutmeat and insects feeding on it. Abundant in California oak woods and many urban areas.

Woodpeckers

Woodpeckers clutch tree bark with extra backward-pointing toe, lean on stiff tail to peck, and explore crevices with stiff, extensible tongue for insects and their eggs. Special jaw suspension absorbs shock of pecking. They chisel nesting cavities in trees, crack nuts, and proclaim territorial rights by pounding resonant branches, trunks, even tin roofs. Call is raspy. Flight is undulating.

Anna's Hummingbird

Other common hummingbirds:

Calliope (streaked, iridescent throat)
Black-chinned (black throat)
Rufous (rusty-colored back)

Head and throat are iridescent red. Rapid, humming wing vibrations involve mostly lengthened outer portion of wings. Motion is like flapping wrists. Inner wing bones (humerus, radius, ulna) are shortened. Has rare ability to fly backwards. Aggressive with other hummingbirds around food source. Eats insects, especially when raising young, but major food is nectar lapped by extensible tongue, usually from bases of red, tube-shaped flowers which only hummingbirds can pollinate—a highly evolved symbiosis. Nest is tiny, deep cup with two eggs made of available fibers, vegetation, moss, lichen. Can be fed on 5:1 water to sugar mixture. Red ribbon on feeder will help attract them.

Western Meadowlark

Black V across bright-yellow chest and loud, clear, melodious song help this prairie bird attract mate and assert its presence to competitors in treeless habitat without high perches. Named after European larks for its song, but more akin to blackbirds. Camouflaged from above by brown-streaked back, it crouches and weaves its way through grass, probing for insects, their eggs, caterpillars, worms and some seeds. Lays five eggs in domed tunnel of grass. Like meadowlark of eastern U.S. except for song.

Evolution of Song

The survival value of bird song goes beyond sex and poetry. Singing birds can threaten encroaching competitors (usually of same species) and encourage them to seek unclaimed territory rather than fight. By avoiding fights, singers save energy for productive foraging, survive better.

American Robin

The best known American bird. Black head and tail, rusty breast. Related to bluebirds and Wood Thrush. Migrates. Very aggressive toward other Robins in spri[n]g when establishing territory. May attack its own image in windows, rear view mirrors, etc. Also hold winter territory. Size of territory is 1/10 to 1/2 acre.

Lays three to five light blue eggs in tree nest made of mud and grass. Young hatch in about two weeks and, like most songbirds, depend on parents for two or thre[e] weeks thereafter.

Western Bluebird

Head, wings and back are blue; throat, breast and sides are rust-colored. Female is much paler. Nests in tree cavities. Eats berries, insects. Spreads mistletoe seeds. Forms winter flocks at low altitudes, often with **Mountain Bluebird** which is striking greenish-blue all over (female paler). When birds pair for breeding, Western Bluebirds occupy low- and middle- elevation woods while Mountain Bluebirds move to sparse woods and meadow edges at high (subalpine) elevations.

Color and Sex-Determined Roles

Most female songbirds are duller than their mates. Colors may help males to advertise presence in territory. But brightness would make nest-sitting females more vulnerable to predators.

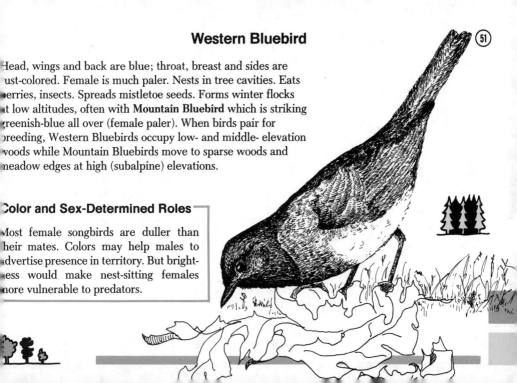

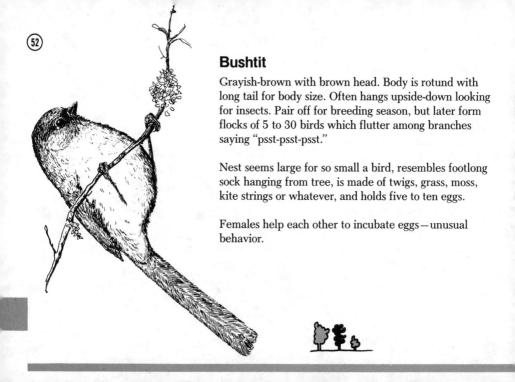

Bushtit

Grayish-brown with brown head. Body is rotund with long tail for body size. Often hangs upside-down looking for insects. Pair off for breeding season, but later form flocks of 5 to 30 birds which flutter among branches saying "psst-psst-psst."

Nest seems large for so small a bird, resembles footlong sock hanging from tree, is made of twigs, grass, moss, kite strings or whatever, and holds five to ten eggs.

Females help each other to incubate eggs—unusual behavior.

Plain Titmouse

Drab, gray, with a short, conical bill and perma-nent topknot. Inhabits lower-elevation woods and parks. Variable, often heard spring song is gen-rally a fast "peter-peter-peter."

Voracious. Eats about one fourth of body weight in in-ects, seeds and berries every day. (Bird metabolism is high, even higher for smaller birds, and burns energy fast.)

Lays six or seven eggs in soft nest of feathers, hair and grass in tree cavity. If either male or female is killed, the other will maintain the terri-ory and try to attract new mate.

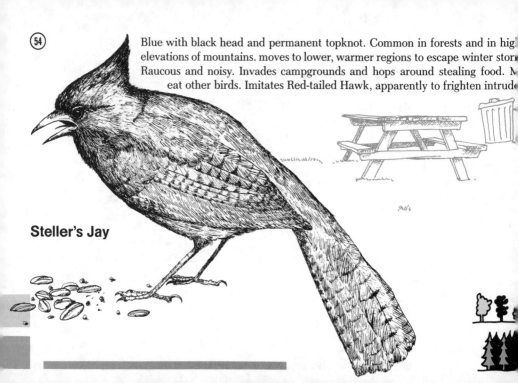

(54)

Blue with black head and permanent topknot. Common in forests and in high
elevations of mountains. moves to lower, warmer regions to escape winter stor[...]
Raucous and noisy. Invades campgrounds and hops around stealing food. M[...]
eat other birds. Imitates Red-tailed Hawk, apparently to frighten intrud[...]

Steller's Jay

Scrub Jay

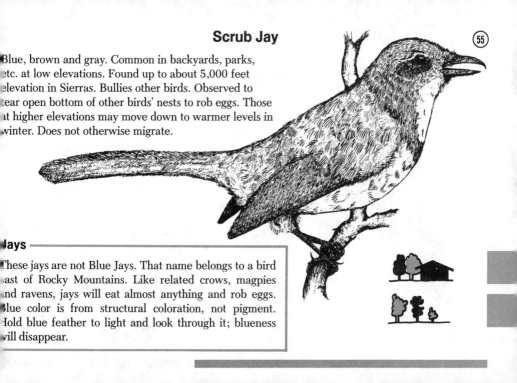

Blue, brown and gray. Common in backyards, parks, etc. at low elevations. Found up to about 5,000 feet elevation in Sierras. Bullies other birds. Observed to tear open bottom of other birds' nests to rob eggs. Those at higher elevations may move down to warmer levels in winter. Does not otherwise migrate.

Jays

These jays are not Blue Jays. That name belongs to a bird east of Rocky Mountains. Like related crows, magpies and ravens, jays will eat almost anything and rob eggs. Blue color is from structural coloration, not pigment. Hold blue feather to light and look through it; blueness will disappear.

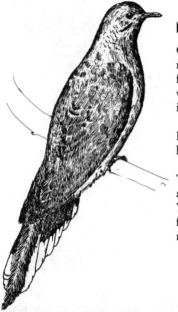

Mourning Dove

Gray-brown, plump-bodied with a pointed tail like its extinct relative, the Passenger Pigeon. Has rapid wing beat and swift flight, but noisy takeoff, especially from ground. Often sits on wires and fences. Plaintive, "mourning" call resembles poorly imitated owl.

Has rare ability to drink by sucking, and need not tilt back head to swallow.

Two eggs are incubated by female during the day and by male at night. Simple, saucer-shaped nest is on or near ground. Young hatch out naked and helpless, are fed with secretion from parent's crop called pigeon's milk. After young leave nest, doves gather in loose flocks of 20 to 30.

Wrens

Small, brownish, with long, thin, downcurved, insect-eating bills, and long, complex, special songs for calling mate, threatening predators, etc. Often sing from exposed perches with tail cocked upright. Nest in tree cavities, wall crevices, branches, marshes. Lay five to seven eggs. Some are polygamous, perhaps due to abundant food which lets females raise young unassisted.

In woods and cities, **House Wren** (shown here) and **Bewick's Wren** (with distinct white stripe over eye) are common. In marshes, **Long-billed Marsh Wren** with white-streaked back is more often heard than seen. Protection of dense vegetation lend courage to sing within few feet of intruders. Nest is spherical with side entrance. Pierces and sucks eggs of Red-winged Blackbirds and other marsh nesters.

Dipper   (Water Ouzel)

Found only in or along swift-running streams. Stays
underwater up to 20 seconds probing for insect larvae
on rocks. Water adaptations include streamlined wings
for underwater flying, thick down for insulation, short
moulting period, and large oil gland at base of tail for
preening oil onto feathers with bill. Flies little. Does n
migrate. Lays three to five eggs in nearly spherical nes
right at water's edge or behind waterfall. Song is complex, flute-like.

White-breasted Nuthatch

Black cap and nape, white chin and undersides, gray body. You can crudely imitate loud call by pinching nose and saying "yeah-yeah-yeah." Most often seen in spiral climb down side of tree, probing bark for insects, their larvae, and spiders. Reaches bottom and flies to top of next tree. Also eats small seeds and nuts. Lays five to eight eggs in tree cavity it finds (or makes, if wood is soft).

Red-Breasted Nuthatch is similar but smaller, with white eye stripe and reddish undersides. Less common **Pygmy Nuthatch** is grayish with brown cap, and is generally restricted to pine forests.

Yellow-rumped Warbler

Has obvious yellow rump patch. Yellow patch on head may or may not be present. The most common Pacific coast warbler. Known formerly as Audubon's Warbler and Myrtle Warbler, now considered one species. Winters in California Central Valley and along coast, and at higher elevations in western states. Breeds in coniferous forests of Canada and Alaska. Generally secretive. Flits rapidly through dense vegetation, hovering and picking insect larvae from twigs, branches and leaves.

Warblers have complex "warbling" songs, and thin bills with strong muscles for closing them on insects and larvae captured in narrow cracks and crevices of bark.

INDEX

Avocet, American 13
Bittern, American 11
Blackbird, Brewer's 32
Blackbird, Red-winged 14
Bluebird, Western 51
Bushtit 52
Coot 15
Cormorant, Double-crested 3
Cowbird, Brown-headed 30
Crow, Common 33
Dipper 58
Dove, Mourning 56
Dove, Rock 34
Ducks 17-19
Egrets 10
Finches 36
Flicker, Common 46
Goose, Canada 21
Grebes 6,7
Grosbeak, Evening 38
Gull, Herring 4
Hawk, Marsh 24
Hawk, Red-tailed 27
Heron, Great Blue 10
Hummingbird, Anna's 48
Jays 54,55
Junco, Dark-eyed 39
Kestrel, American 25
Kildeer 12

Kingbird, Western 28
Kingfisher, Belted 8
Magpie, Yellow-billed 31
Mallard 18
Meadowlark, Western 49
Mockingbird 43
Nighthawk, Common 45
Nuthatch, White-breasted 59
Owl, Barn 44
Pelicans 2
Pheasant, Ring-necked 22
Pigeon 34
Pintail 19
Quail, California 23
Robin, American 50
Sandpiper, Spotted 9
Shrike, Loggerhead 42
Sparrow, House 35
Sparrow, White-crowned 37
Starling 35
Swallow, Barn 29
Swan Whistling 20
Tern, Black 5
Titmouse, Plain 53
Towhee, Rufous-sided 40
Vulture, Turkey 26
Warbler, Yellow-rumped 60
Waxwing, Cedar 41
Woodpeckers 46,47
Wrens 57

Other books in the pocket-sized "finder" series:

for U.S. and Canada east of the Rockies

TREE FINDER - native and common introduced trees
FLOWER FINDER - spring wildflowers & flower families
WINTER TREE FINDER - leafless winter trees
FERN FINDER - native ferns of the Midwest and Northeast
TRACK FINDER - tracks and footprints of mammals
BERRY FINDER - native plants with fleshy fruits
LIFE ON INTERTIDAL ROCKS - organisms of North Atlantic coast
BIRD FINDER - some common birds and how they live
WINTER WEED FINDER - dry plant structures in winter

for the Pacific Coast

PACIFIC COAST TREE FINDER - native trees, Sitka to San Diego
PACIFIC COAST BIRD FINDER - common birds and their habitats
PACIFIC COAST BERRY FINDER - native plants with fleshy fruits
REDWOOD REGION FLOWER FINDER - wildflowers of the coastal fog belt
SIERRA FLOWER FINDER - wildflowers of the Sierra Nevada
PACIFIC INTERTIDAL LIFE - organisms of tidepools, rocks and reefs
PACIFIC COAST FERN FINDER - native ferns and fern relatives
PACIFIC COAST MAMMALS - mammals, their tracks, other signs
PACIFIC COAST FISH - marine fish, Alaska to Mexico

for Rocky Mt. and desert states

ROCKY MOUNTAIN TREE FINDER - native Rocky Mountain trees
DESERT TREE FINDER - desert trees of CA, AZ, NM
ROCKY MOUNTAIN FLOWER FINDER - wildflowers below tree line
MOUNTAIN STATE MAMMALS - mammals, their tracks, skulls, scat

NATURE STUDY GUILD PUBLISHERS, Box 10489, Rochester, NY 14610, **www.naturestudy.com**